D1372099

We would like to thank the editorial board, Martine Laffon, Catherine Peugeot and Alba Zamolo, for their clarity, professionalism and enthusiasm. More particularly, we are grateful to Catherine for her great competence and friendly support in the fine-tuning of the text and the titles.

Thanks to Annie Madec who supervised the iconography, which the authors kept modifying, with great efficiency and good humour.

Thanks to Céline Julhiet-Charvet who oversaw the production of this book, until Fanny arrived on the scene.

Thanks to Chloé Demey who took over briskly from Céline.

Thanks to Frédéric Célestin who generously gave his time to the conception, adaptation and polishing of the page lay out.

Thanks to Anne de Margerie who was behind the original idea for the project, and to Béatrice Foulon who encouraged it with enthusiasm.

Thanks to Jean Galard for his sharp eye.

Thanks to Karine Barou, Hugues Charreyron, Annick Duboscq and all the others who shared in this journey to the heart of the Louvre.

For Vianney, Flamine, Julien, Baptiste, Pierre and Dora.

Graphics and lay-out by Frédéric Célestin
Adapted by Christiane Charlot
English translation by Anna-Louise Milne

© Éditions de la Réunion des musées nationaux, 1999
   49, rue Étienne-Marcel
   75001 Paris
   ISBN : 2-7118-3973-7

Cynthia E. Daugherty
55 Fuller Dr.
Carrollton, GA 30117-9649

Wonders of the Louvre

•

Marie Sellier

•

Violaine Bouvet-Lanselle

Réunion
des Musées
Nationaux

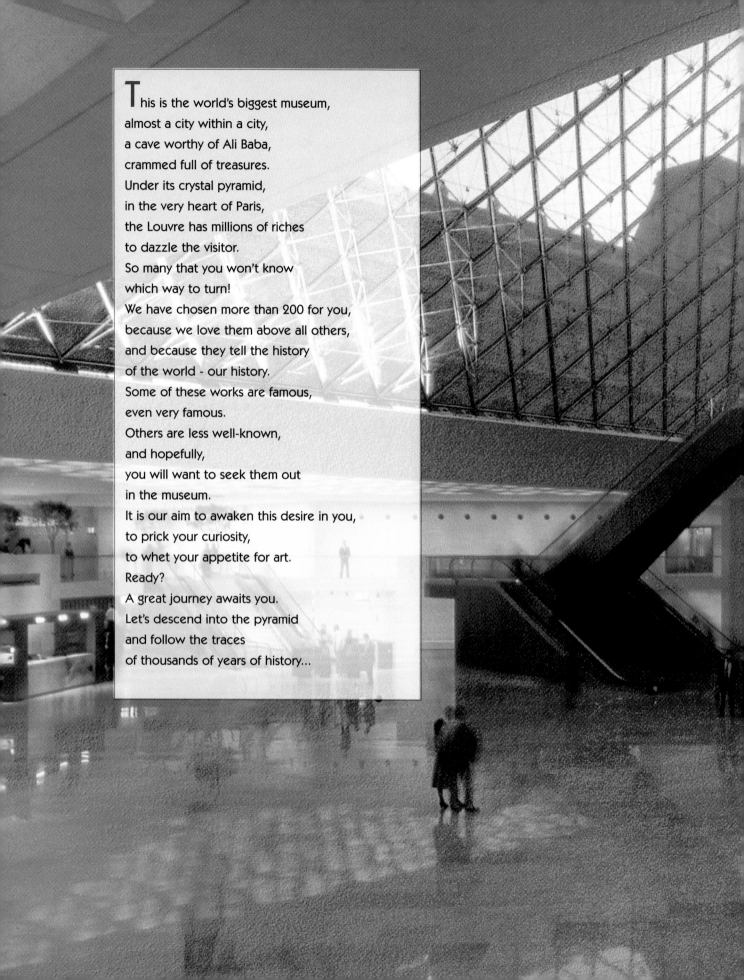

This is the world's biggest museum,
almost a city within a city,
a cave worthy of Ali Baba,
crammed full of treasures.
Under its crystal pyramid,
in the very heart of Paris,
the Louvre has millions of riches
to dazzle the visitor.
So many that you won't know
which way to turn!
We have chosen more than 200 for you,
because we love them above all others,
and because they tell the history
of the world - our history.
Some of these works are famous,
even very famous.
Others are less well-known,
and hopefully,
you will want to seek them out
in the museum.
It is our aim to awaken this desire in you,
to prick your curiosity,
to whet your appetite for art.
Ready?
A great journey awaits you.
Let's descend into the pyramid
and follow the traces
of thousands of years of history...

ANCIENT ORIENT

Mysterious Mesopotamia

Everything began in Mesopotamia more than 10 000 years ago. There, between the Tigris and the Euphrates, known as "the land between two rivers," the world's oldest civilisation was born. Gradually the people gathered villages, tamed wild animals and started to sow grain. Later they invented writing. Over thousands of years Mesopotamian civilisation developed its incredible splendor, which still shines for us today like a mysterious star.

Neolithic Statuette, beginning of the 6th Millennium BC

An Amazing Ancestor

This tiny little alabaster woman is the oldest statue in the Louvre. It was found in a vault under the floor of a house. Her rounded forms suggest that she was a mother-goddess who brought fertility to the land and the women.

Ebih II, the Superintendent, c. 2400 BC

Tablet of pre-cuneiform writing, 3rd Millennium BC

The First Writing

This clay tablet records the women, crops and cows belonging to one village or local lord. These engraved pictograms are the first form of writing.

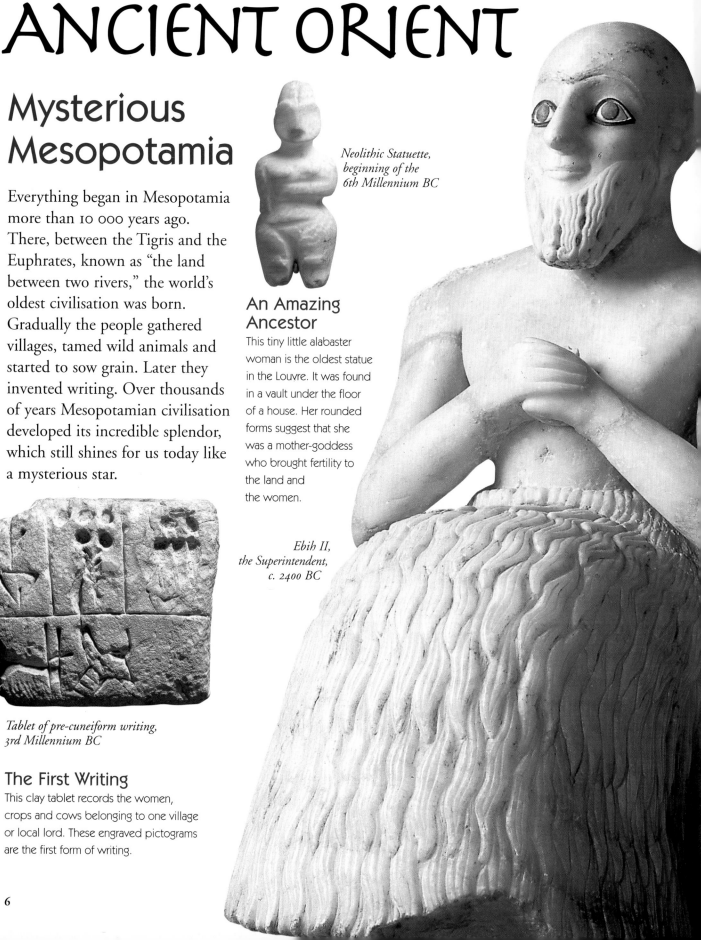

6

Gudea,
Prince of Lagash,
c. 2150 BC

Gudea with
Overflowing Vase,
c. 2120 BC

Law-Codex of
Hammurabi,
c. 1750 BC

Gudea Seated,
c. 2120 BC

◄ An Everlasting Smile

The Superintendent Ebih II was such
an important person that in one temple
his statue was placed in front of that
of the Mother Goddess. His ceremonial
skirt was made of sheepskin. Here he is
in prayer, with his hands crossed and
a contemplative gaze.

The Youthful Prince

The young prince Gudea looks very
composed under his large brimmed hat.
He is shown sitting and standing, with
his hands joined in prayer or clasped
around a vase from which springs the
water of life... The Louvre has some
twenty statues of this prince who
reigned over the kingdom of Lagash.

Written in Stone

Hammurabi was the powerful king
of Babylon. He had his laws
engraved on huge stones and
placed in every city of his kingdom
so that no-one could forget his
authority. He is shown above the
3000 lines of text face to face with
Shamash, the sun-god.

The Terrifying Assyrians

One powerful empire dominated Mesopotamian history: the Assyrian empire. The Assyrians were bloodthirsty warriors, and their kings were terribly ambitious. They built immense palaces whose beauties and riches surpass all imagination. In fact, the palace of Sargon II in Khorsabad was a town in itself.

The Jaws of the Lion

What a strange jug! The water is poured through the lion's mouth. It was found a long way from Mesopotamia, in Turkey, where it had been taken by a rich Assyrian merchant.

Gigantic Angels

This winged giant with muscular calves is a guardian angel. He blesses the king's palace with a cedar apple which he first dips into a bucket of precious water.

Lion-Shaped Vase, c. 1950–1750 BC

Genie, Palace of Assurnairpal II, c. 865 BC

King of Demons

On the little bronze statue's back we can read: "I am Pazuzu, son of Hampa, the king of demons. I am the winds that sweep down from the mountains, creating a frenzy." The Assyrians believed in all number of gods and genii, good and bad. And some were both good and bad. Pazuzu, for example, was also called upon to drive away sickness!

▼

The Demon Pazuzu, c. 900 BC

Winged Assyrian Bull, c. 720 BC

On All Five Legs

These gigantic bulls with human heads protected the entrance to the palace of Sargon II at Khorsabad. Their triking feature is their five feet, which allow them to be seen as well in profile as from the front, in movement and at rest. Each one weighs over 3 tons. Bringing them to the Louvre was a truly gigantic feat!

9

Splendid Persia

To the east of Mesopotamia, Persian Empire spread its brilliance across the whole of the Orient. 2 500 years ago Darius I proclaimed himself "the King of Kings." His monumental and luxurious palace at Susa was decorated in great style. Nothing was too beautiful for Darius the Magnificent.

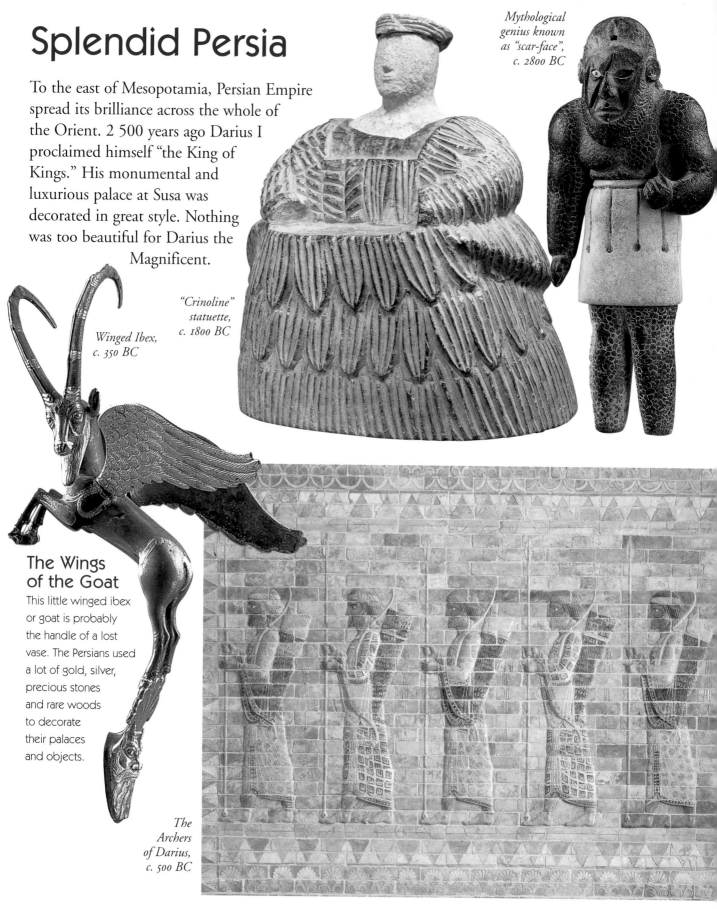

Mythological genius known as "scar-face", c. 2800 BC

"Crinoline" statuette, c. 1800 BC

Winged Ibex, c. 350 BC

The Wings of the Goat

This little winged ibex or goat is probably the handle of a lost vase. The Persians used a lot of gold, silver, precious stones and rare woods to decorate their palaces and objects.

The Archers of Darius, c. 500 BC

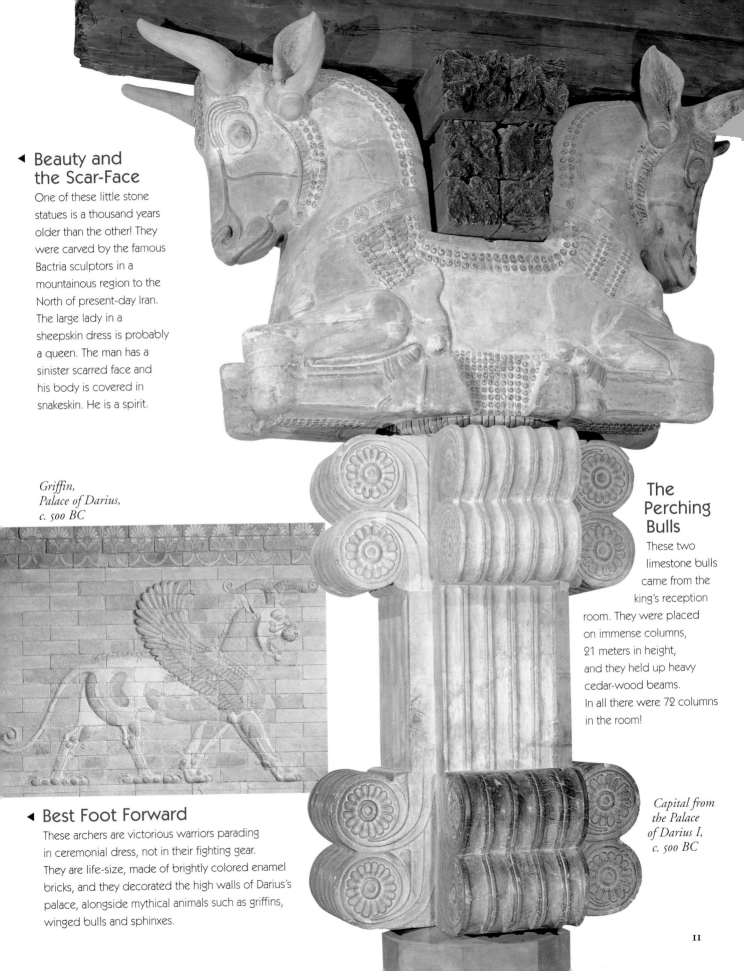

◄ Beauty and the Scar-Face

One of these little stone statues is a thousand years older than the other! They were carved by the famous Bactria sculptors in a mountainous region to the North of present-day Iran. The large lady in a sheepskin dress is probably a queen. The man has a sinister scarred face and his body is covered in snakeskin. He is a spirit.

Griffin,
Palace of Darius,
c. 500 BC

The Perching Bulls

These two limestone bulls came from the king's reception room. They were placed on immense columns, 21 meters in height, and they held up heavy cedar-wood beams. In all there were 72 columns in the room!

◄ Best Foot Forward

These archers are victorious warriors parading in ceremonial dress, not in their fighting gear. They are life-size, made of brightly colored enamel bricks, and they decorated the high walls of Darius's palace, alongside mythical animals such as griffins, winged bulls and sphinxes.

Capital from the Palace of Darius I, c. 500 BC

11

Egypt

The Gods Take the Lead

Let's leave ancient Orient and move on to the fascinating universe of ancient Egypt. This civilization, which lasted over 3 000 years, is like no other. Its gods were numerous and all powerful. The fact that the sun rose and set each day depended on the gods. It was only by the grace of the gods that the Nile flowed abundantly each year, and that children were born. The Egyptians built huge temples and filled them with statues to secure divine protection. The king of Egypt, the pharaoh, was himself a god on earth.

Blue Head, between 1400 and 1340 BC

Toutankhamen

This tiny head is 9 centimeters tall. It is made of glass paste and almost certainly represents the young pharaoh Toutankhamen, who reigned for just a few years. His mausoleum is one of the rare ones to have been found intact with all its treasures.

The Chopped-Up God

Osiris is the god of the underworld, and he is wrapped up in a shroud like a mummy. There is a good reason for this: he was killed and cut into pieces by his brother Seth. His wife, Isis, enabled him to recover his powers. ▶

A Great Magician

Isis was such a great magician that she succeeded in piecing her husband Osiris together after he was chopped up by his jealous brother.

Statuette of Isis, stuccoed wood, 4th-1st century BC

Statuette of Taharqa adoring the Falcon God, c. 700 BC

Kneeling Before the Falcon God

This little kneeling man is the powerful pharaoh Taharqa. He is making an offering to the falcon god.

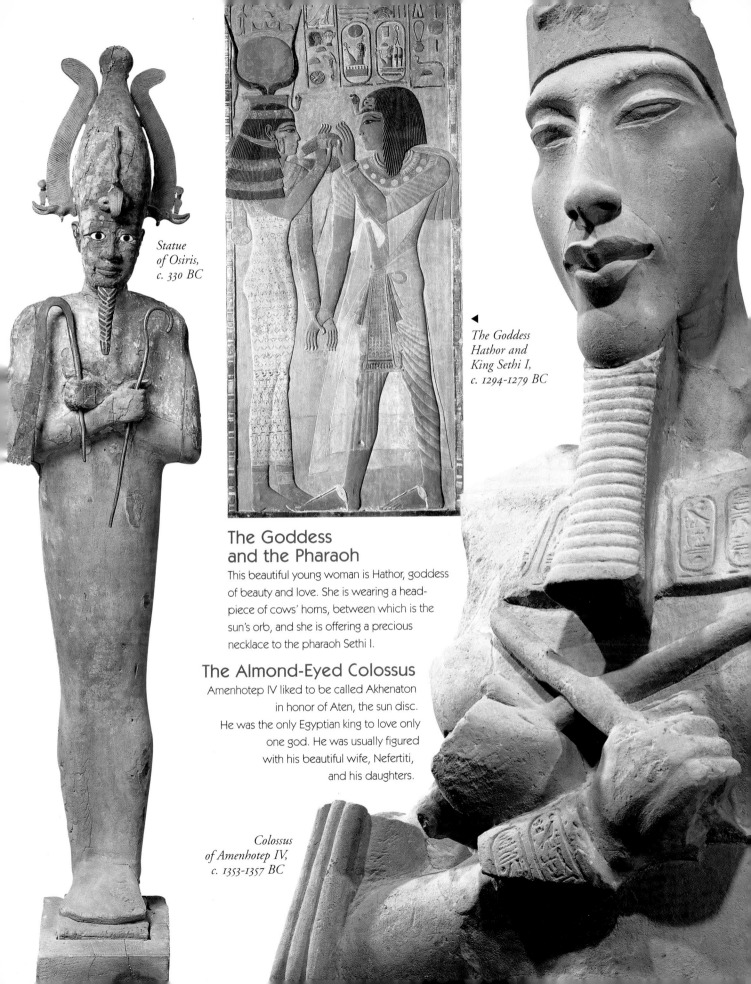

Statue of Osiris, c. 330 BC

The Goddess Hathor and King Sethi I, c. 1294-1279 BC

The Goddess and the Pharaoh

This beautiful young woman is Hathor, goddess of beauty and love. She is wearing a head-piece of cows' horns, between which is the sun's orb, and she is offering a precious necklace to the pharaoh Sethi I.

The Almond-Eyed Colossus

Amenhotep IV liked to be called Akhenaton in honor of Aten, the sun disc. He was the only Egyptian king to love only one god. He was usually figured with his beautiful wife, Nefertiti, and his daughters.

Colossus of Amenhotep IV, c. 1353-1357 BC

Living and Dying on the Banks of the Nile

The Egyptians thought that life in the hereafter was the same as on earth. But just in case they felt a little lost they decorated their tombs with scenes from everyday life, a bit like a comic strip. They were also buried with all their familiar objects. Today, the paintings, statues and objects found in the tombs enable us to imagine how the Egyptians lived 3 000 years ago.

In the Same Basket

These baskets look like they were used only yesterday, but in fact they are over 3 500 years old! The very dry air in the tombs kept them intact. Similar baskets are still used today.

Three baskets, c. 1786-1555 BC

To Work ▶

Here an unknown artist has shown in detail how the land was labored, from sowing to harvesting. This was how most Egyptians lived: 9 out of 10 were peasants at the time.

Heaps of Hippopotamuses

In ancient Egyptian times the Nile was full of hippopotamuses. These glazed earthenware ones are painted in the blue of the great river that ensured Egypt's wealth. Each year the Nile flooded leaving a very fertile black silt on its banks.

Hippopotamuses, c. 2000-1900 BC

Model of a boat, from the tomb of Chancellor Nakhti, c. 2000-1800 BC

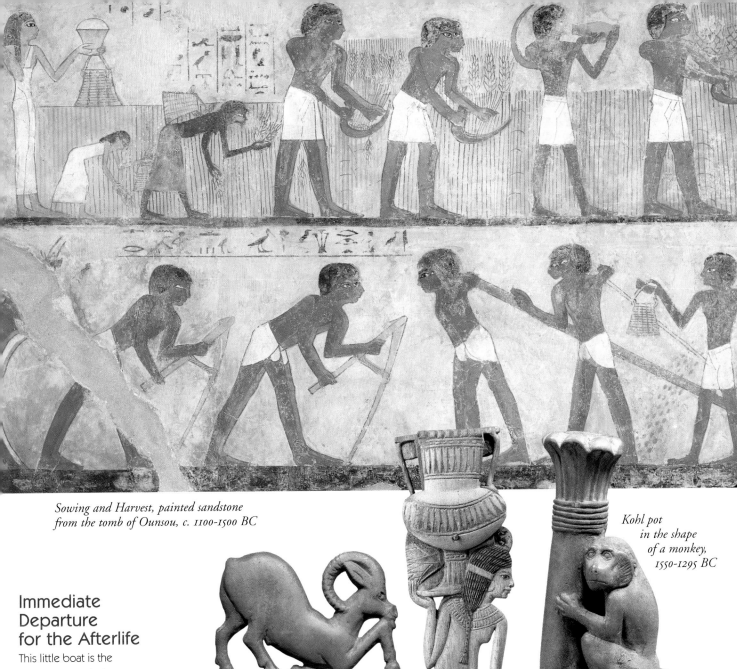

*Sowing and Harvest, painted sandstone
from the tomb of Ounsou, c. 1100-1500 BC*

*Kohl pot
in the shape
of a monkey,
1550-1295 BC*

Immediate Departure for the Afterlife

This little boat is the size of a toy. It is the exact replica of the boats that navigated the Nile. Its owner would continue to sail on the river after his death.

Ibex comb, c. 1555-1080 BC

*Make-up spatula with
a young girl carrying
a vase, c. 1400-1360 BC*

Beauty Accessories

Ordinary cosmetic objects were transformed by craftsmen into true works of art. A wooden comb is decorated with a life-like little ibex, a tiny monkey holds on to a small kohl pot, and a wooden make-up spatula is transformed into an exquisite sculpture.

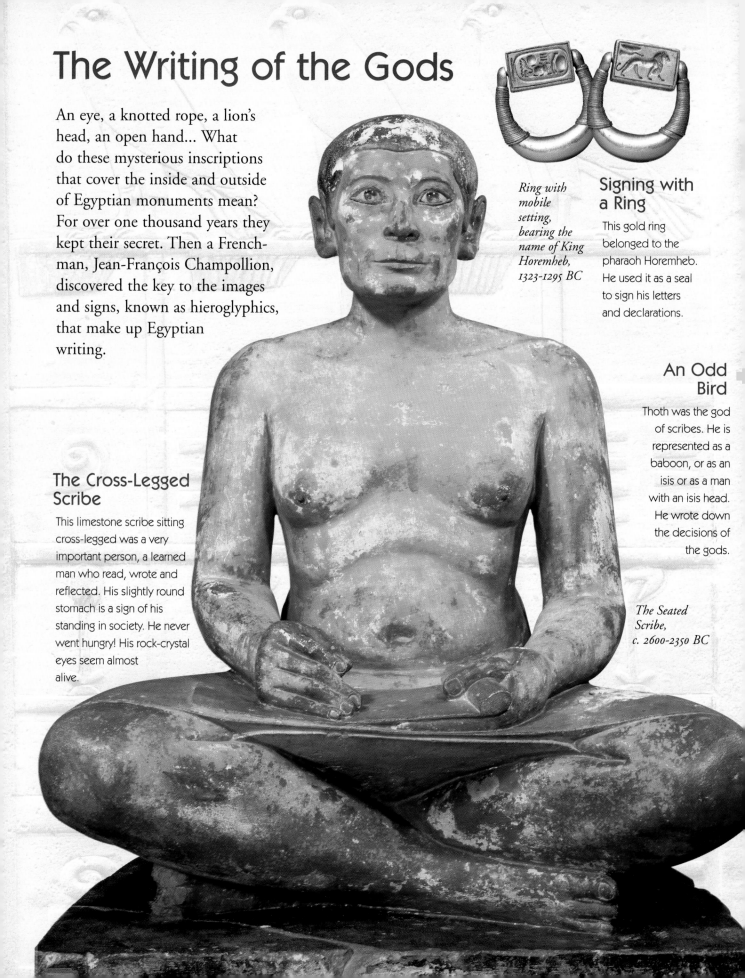

The Writing of the Gods

An eye, a knotted rope, a lion's head, an open hand... What do these mysterious inscriptions that cover the inside and outside of Egyptian monuments mean? For over one thousand years they kept their secret. Then a Frenchman, Jean-François Champollion, discovered the key to the images and signs, known as hieroglyphics, that make up Egyptian writing.

Ring with mobile setting, bearing the name of King Horemheb, 1323-1295 BC

Signing with a Ring

This gold ring belonged to the pharaoh Horemheb. He used it as a seal to sign his letters and declarations.

An Odd Bird

Thoth was the god of scribes. He is represented as a baboon, or as an isis or as a man with an isis head. He wrote down the decisions of the gods.

The Cross-Legged Scribe

This limestone scribe sitting cross-legged was a very important person, a learned man who read, wrote and reflected. His slightly round stomach is a sign of his standing in society. He never went hungry! His rock-crystal eyes seem almost alive.

The Seated Scribe, c. 2600-2350 BC

The god Thoth with an ibis head, holding the eye of Oudjat, c. 664-332 BC

▲ *Stele of Nefertiabet, c. 2590 BC*

In the Name of the King!

When a stylized rope forms an oval loop around a group of hieroglyphics then we know this signifies the name of a king. It is called a cartouche. This is the cartouche for Sethi I, who was the father of Ramses II.

Cartouche of Sethi I, 1304-1290 BC

Picture Words

There are more than 700 hieroglyphics. Some are the picture of what they mean (a picture of a duck means "duck"), and are called ideograms. The others represent sounds and are called phonograms.

Palette, pot and papyrus knife, 1550-1295 BC

A Writer's Kit

The word paper comes from "papyrus," which is a riverbed plant. It was carefully dried and prepared for the scribes to write upon.

17

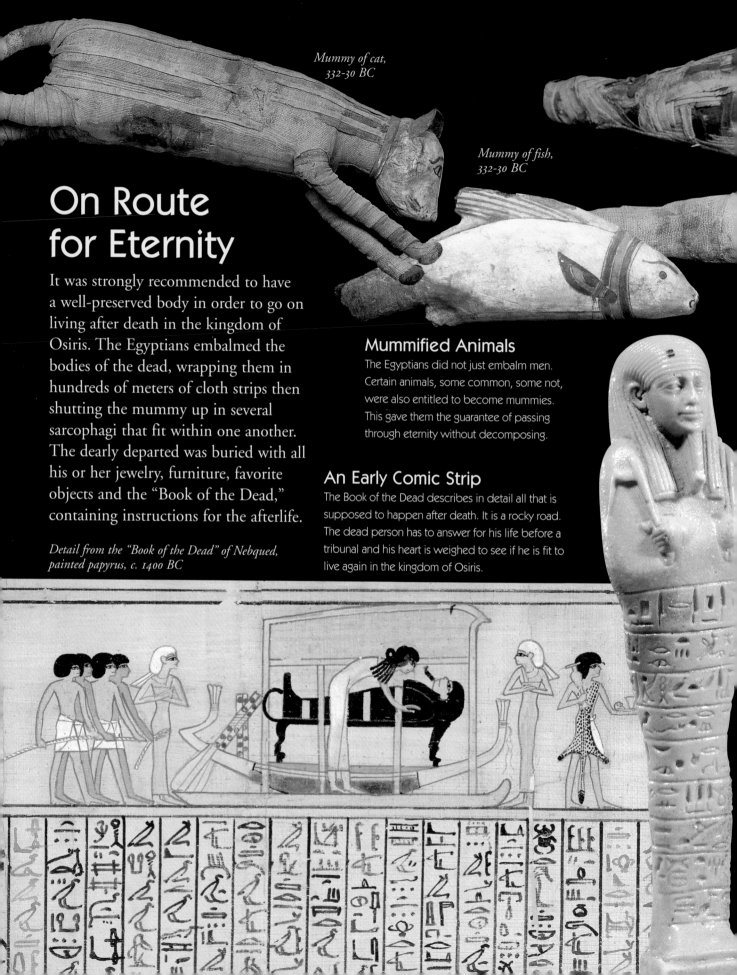

Mummy of cat,
332-30 BC

Mummy of fish,
332-30 BC

On Route for Eternity

It was strongly recommended to have a well-preserved body in order to go on living after death in the kingdom of Osiris. The Egyptians embalmed the bodies of the dead, wrapping them in hundreds of meters of cloth strips then shutting the mummy up in several sarcophagi that fit within one another. The dearly departed was buried with all his or her jewelry, furniture, favorite objects and the "Book of the Dead," containing instructions for the afterlife.

Detail from the "Book of the Dead" of Nebqued,
painted papyrus, c. 1400 BC

Mummified Animals

The Egyptians did not just embalm men. Certain animals, some common, some not, were also entitled to become mummies. This gave them the guarantee of passing through eternity without decomposing.

An Early Comic Strip

The Book of the Dead describes in detail all that is supposed to happen after death. It is a rocky road. The dead person has to answer for his life before a tribunal and his heart is weighed to see if he is fit to live again in the kingdom of Osiris.

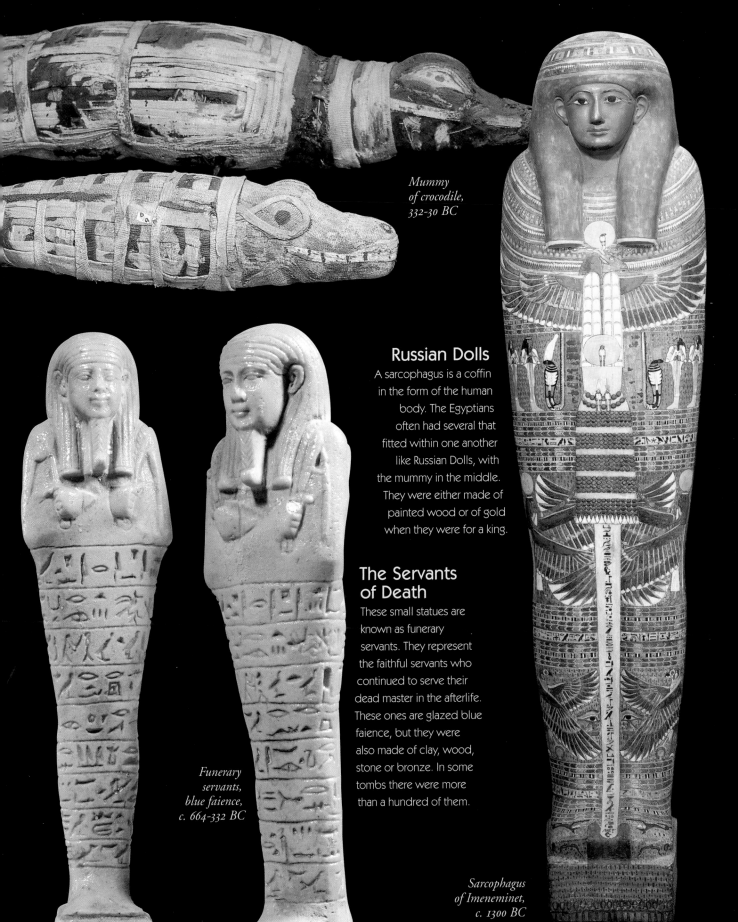

Mummy of crocodile, 332-30 BC

Russian Dolls

A sarcophagus is a coffin in the form of the human body. The Egyptians often had several that fitted within one another like Russian Dolls, with the mummy in the middle. They were either made of painted wood or of gold when they were for a king.

The Servants of Death

These small statues are known as funerary servants. They represent the faithful servants who continued to serve their dead master in the afterlife. These ones are glazed blue faience, but they were also made of clay, wood, stone or bronze. In some tombs there were more than a hundred of them.

Funerary servants, blue faience, c. 664-332 BC

Sarcophagus of Imeneminet, c. 1300 BC

GREECE

Who Rules on Mount Olympus?

Time to stop off in ancient Greece, the land of the gods! Their statues describe their fantastic life-stories in detail. They may be immortal, but they still have an age: they are 3000 years old! They lived almost like humans, laughing, fighting and falling in love... They were sensitive, sharp and jealous. They gathered on Mount Olympus, one of the highest mountains in their land. Later the Romans made these gods their own, but gave them different names.

The Judgment of Paris,
Antioch (Turkey), 115 AD

ZEUS
JUPITER

King of the Gods, enthroned upon Mount Olympus. He commanded the storms and the rain. He had a troubled love-life, always falling in love with mere mortals. His emblem is his thunder-bolt.

Statuette of Zeus,
Roman period

HADES
PLUTO

Another brother of Zeus. Rarely left the underworld. Often represented in the act of abducting Persephone (Proserpina), his future wife. His emblem is a giant staff.

HERA - JUNO

Zeus's wife. She was always fighting with her unfaithful husband. She couldn't stand the idea that Paris found Aphrodite more beautiful than her. Her favorite animal was the pheasant.

Athena
the Peaceful,
2nd century AD

ATHENA
MINERVA

Goddess of wisdom and reason, she was born from the head of Zeus. She counseled warriors. Her emblems are her head-dress, her lance and her shield.

Hades and Persephone,
Red Figure Amphora,
c. 479 BC

Mosaic: Triumph of
Neptune and Amphitrite,
c. 315-325 AD

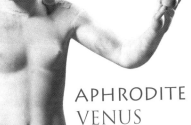

Ceramic Krater:
the Return of Hephaistos,
c. 525 BC

HERMES
MERCURY

Son of Zeus. Messenger
of the gods because he was
so fast and cunning.
Distinguished
by his cap
and his
winged
sandals. ▶

HEPHAISTOS
VULCAN

Son of Zeus. He was
so ugly at birth that his
mother, Hera, threw him
from the top of Olympus.
He was left lame from
this experience. God of
metal-working, who
supplied weapons and
tools of all sorts. Married
to the beautiful
Aphrodite.

APHRODITE
VENUS

A true beauty,
born from the froth
of the sea. Goddess
of love and beauty.
She sowed passion
with her son Eros,
a baby armed with
a bow and arrows.

POSEIDON ▲
NEPTUNE

Brother of Zeus. God of the sea,
married to Amphitrite, a nymph.

Statuette
of Hermes,
c. 450 BC

Couple as
Mars and
Venus,
c. 150 BC

Aphrodite of Cnidus,
c. 320 BC

Diana
of Versailles,
c. 50 BC

There is one missing... which one?
Turn the page to find out...

ARES
MARS

Son of Zeus. God
of war. Became very
aggressive when in
love. Had a love affair
with Aphrodite, his
sister-in-law.
Recognizable by his
helmet and his weapons.

ARTEMIS
DIANA

Daughter of Zeus.
Goddess of hunting.
Recognizable by
her crown with
a crescent moon,
her bow, her quiver and
the deer or dog that
accompanies her.

Getting to Know Apollo

Apollo is the eternal young man, god of beauty, the arts and poetry. He is the son of Zeus and the mortal Leto, and his twin sister is Artemis. In memory of the nymph Daphne, whom he cherished, he often wears a crown of laurels. He is frequently the model for statues of male nudes.

Head of a Horseman, Athens, c. 559 BC

A Dashing Stranger

Who is this fine horseman? Is it Apollo, Castor, Pollux or a noble Athenian wearing a crown won in a sporting competition? Whoever it is, he took good care of his beard and his hairstyle, which is formed of a mass of tiny beads.

Kouros, found at Actium, c. 579 BC

The Man of Marble

This young man seems rather stiff with his arms pinned against his side and his left leg slightly forward. But this was the way the Archaic sculptors represented man in the image of an idealized Apollo.

The Piombino Apollo, 1st century BC or AD

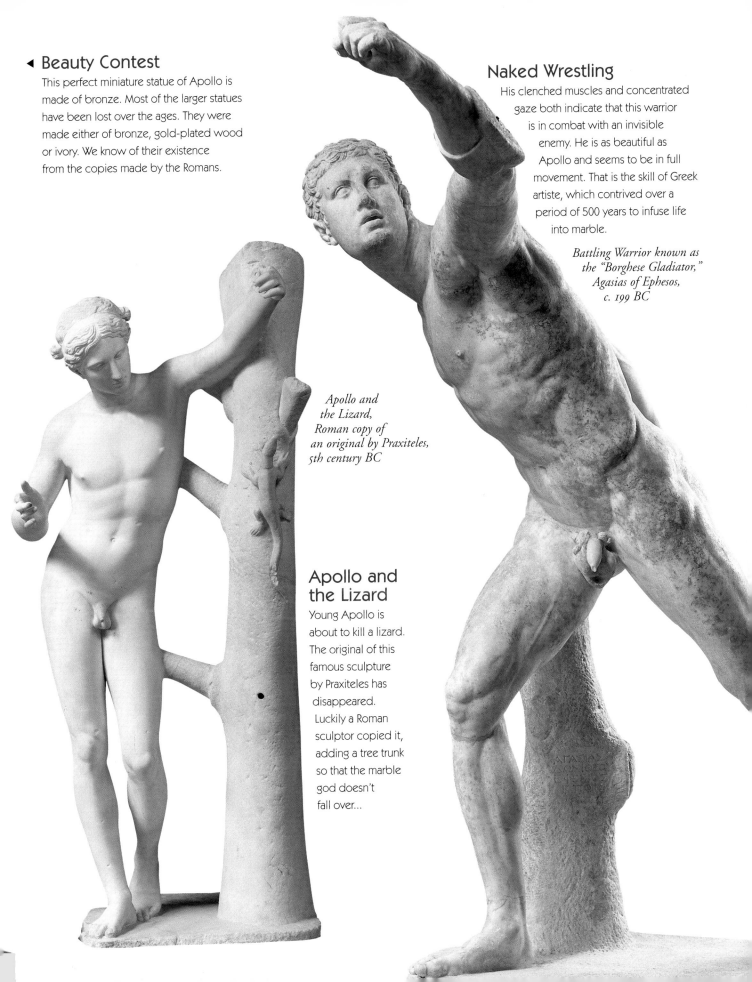

◄ Beauty Contest

This perfect miniature statue of Apollo is made of bronze. Most of the larger statues have been lost over the ages. They were made either of bronze, gold-plated wood or ivory. We know of their existence from the copies made by the Romans.

Naked Wrestling

His clenched muscles and concentrated gaze both indicate that this warrior is in combat with an invisible enemy. He is as beautiful as Apollo and seems to be in full movement. That is the skill of Greek artiste, which contrived over a period of 500 years to infuse life into marble.

Battling Warrior known as the "Borghese Gladiator," Agasias of Ephesos, c. 199 BC

Apollo and the Lizard, Roman copy of an original by Praxiteles, 5th century BC

Apollo and the Lizard

Young Apollo is about to kill a lizard. The original of this famous sculpture by Praxiteles has disappeared. Luckily a Roman sculptor copied it, adding a tree trunk so that the marble god doesn't fall over...

Hercules is the Strongest of All

Son of Zeus and the queen Alcmene, Hercules is the best known Greek hero. Jupiter's wife, Juno, was terribly jealous of him and she inflicted all sorts of trials upon him, the most famous being the twelve labors. Hercules came to a sorry end: his wife, Dejanire, punished him for his infidelity by giving him a poisoned tunic. It burnt his skin so dreadfully that he asked his friends to burn him alive. After his death Zeus gave the order to welcome him into the kingdom of the gods.

*Red Figure
Footed Krater,
Hercules and Antaeus,
c. 510 BC*

Fight to the Death

Antaeus was a terrible giant who spent his time fighting. He won every time since he was invincible as long as he touched the ground. Hercules alone managed to lift him up and strangle him. The painter Euphronios depicted this intense battle using the new technique called "red figure" painting. The background is painted black but the figures remained red, the color of the terracotta.

God, They're Gorgeous!

The Greeks offered statues to their gods to win their good favor. They used to carve beautiful women in the purest marble. The workmanship of the sculptors is quite remarkable. They polished the hard marble endlessly to achieve the soft texture of skin, and they draped the folds of cloth neatly and gracefully.

*Winged
Victory of
Samothrace,
c. 199 BC*

*Venus
de Milo,
c. 199 BC*

Goddess of love

Aphrodite's body is perfectly proportioned. The flowing movement embodied in this sculpture characterizes the Hellenistic period, which followed the Archaic and Classical periods.

On the Wings of Victory

With her open wings and her tunic flattened by sea spray, Victory of Samothrace is an awe-inspiring celebration of a battle won by the inhabitants of the island of Rhodes. She originally stood looking out over the sea.

Hand on my Heart

This gently smiling little woman, with her hair styled like an Egyptian and a richly embroidered dress, is saying her prayers. She combines Greek influences with those of the Orient. She was found on Crete, where the Greeks had founded a colony.

Kore of Samos, c. 579-569 BC

Fresh Faced

A large oval and a small cone are all it takes to form this idol's face. It seems very modern, but it is actually about 4500 years old! It was part of a 1.5 meters heigh statue, which was exceptionally tall for the period.

Female Head, Cyclades, 2799-2399 BC

Dame d'Auxerre, c. 639 BC

Archaic Beauty

This statue of a young girl, dressed in a long, folded tunic and a wool mantle, was offered to the goddess Hera. She is standing stiffly, as is typical of sculpture from the Archaic period, the oldest period in Greek art.

Classical Young Girls

These of young girls are bringing a tunic they have made to the goddess Athena. Their dresses fall in the sort of folds that classical sculptors loved to carve in the era of Pericles. This scene is a fragment of a decorative panel from the Parthenon.

Plaque from the Parthenon Frieze, c. 440 BC

Games For All Ages

Leisure activities represented an important part of Greek life. Children's toys, like jacks, animals on wheels and dolls, are the same today. Adult games were often, however, much more brutal.

The Goose Game

This little boy is playing with a goose that he has perhaps tamed. They are both remarkably life-like. The sculptors of this period often represented children.

Child and Goose, Roman copy from a Greek original from 3rd century BC

Gladiators' Armor, 1st century AD: head-piece, greaves

Playing Nasty

Before fighting with their bare fists, the gladiators used to parade in the arena dressed in sumptuous armor. This head-piece and the greaves that protected the legs are decorated with a Gorgon whose terrible stare turns the opponent to stone.

Dining While Reclining

The rich Greeks used to lie down to eat during their great banquets. They didn't just eat and drink. They also held philosophical debates, recited poetry and sang... In other words, they had a fine old time.

Black Figure Corinthian Krater, c. 569 BC

*Jacks Box
in the form of
Hercules' head,
terracotta,
Asia minor,
c. 59 BC*

back

front

A Box of Jacks

This was and still is one of
the favorite games of Greek
children. The tiny jacks were
stored in a drawer at the
back of a bust of the hero
Hercules.

Treasured Doll

The arms and legs
of this doll can move,
which makes it all the
more fun to play with.
When the little girl
who treasured her doll
grew up, she offered it
to a goddess.

A Buffalo
on Wheels

Like all children learning to walk,
babies in ancient Greece liked to
pull a wheeled toy behind them.
This one was found in a tomb.

*Buffalo on Wheels,
Greater Greece,
Archaic Period*

*Doll,
Taranto,
3rd century BC*

29

ROME

Etruscans and Romans

Altar of Domitius Ahenobarbus, Scenes from a Census, c. 100 BC

Following our journey around the Mediterranean, we arrive in Italy, home of the Etruscans. Long before the Romans, the Etruscan artists could sculpt stone and model clay with great skill. After the foundation of Rome in 753 BC, Roman culture grew in stature. It didn't take the Romans long to establish their art. They were particularly strong on portraits and low reliefs.

Sacrifice

Mars, the god of war, used to receive a bull, a ram and a pig in sacrifice. This ceremony was repeated every four years, when citizens were recruited into the army.

Emperor Nero, 1st century AD

Augustus of Cerveteri, c. 50 AD

Portrait of Livia, c. 30 BC

August Augustus

Emperor Augustus often had his portrait done. He sent these sculptures out to the provinces so that his people knew that he was their supreme leader. He left such a mark on the minds of the Romans that they continued to sculpt his face after his death. This is an example of posthumous portraiture.

Imperial Livia

Carved in the hard stone of basalt, the features of empress Livia, wife of Augustus, have a metallic look. She seems very determined. The knot of hair on her forehead and the low bun were both fashionable hairstyles at the beginning of the Empire.

◄ Hell and Hellfire

The image we now have of Nero is of a despotic and decadent emperor. He was responsible for the fire of Rome. He was consigned to history after his assassination in 68. His portraits were destroyed. This one escaped destruction because it comes from Cilicia, a province remote from Rome.

An Etruscan Couple

The man and woman reclining on a bed are offering one another wine and perfume. They are guests at a typical banquet of the day. These wonderful life-size figures decorated their coffin. It is unequaled in the world for its size and its beauty.

Sarcophagus of a Married Couple, c. 520-510 BC

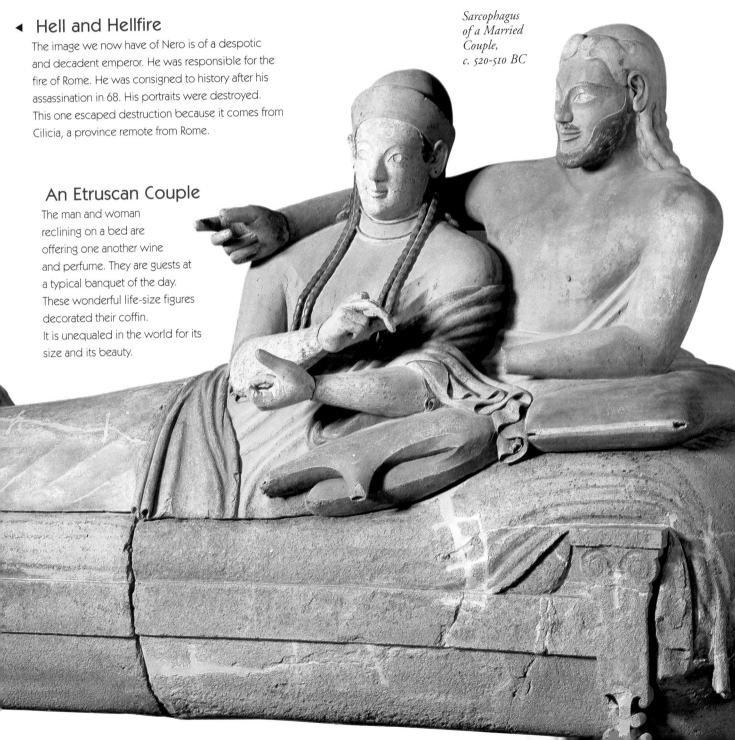

Life in Rome

When the Romans weren't at war, they liked to amuse themselves and decorate their homes. Games played an important role in their life, and they were particularly fond of chariot races, gladiator and wrestling matches, and wild game hunts. Rich Romans had frescoes painted on the walls of their homes and mosaics fitted into the floors.

Roman Boxing

Roman wrestlers were the ancestors of modern boxers, but they fought with bare fists. This game is called a "pancratium" and it was one of the Romans' most popular pastimes. This bronze wrestler has been captured by the artist just as he kicked out at his opponent.

Cup Decorated by Skeletons, Boscoreale, end of 1st century BC

Gruesome Goblets

109 pieces of gold and silver tableware were found in a hiding place where they had been buried by a family fleeing the fatal lava of Vesuvius. The skeletons on this goblet prefigure the tragic fate of their unlucky owner.

Wrestler, 1st century AD, bronze

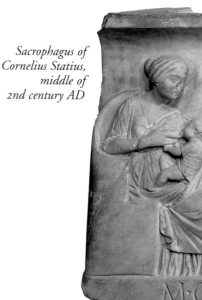

Sacrophagus of Cornelius Statius, middle of 2nd century AD

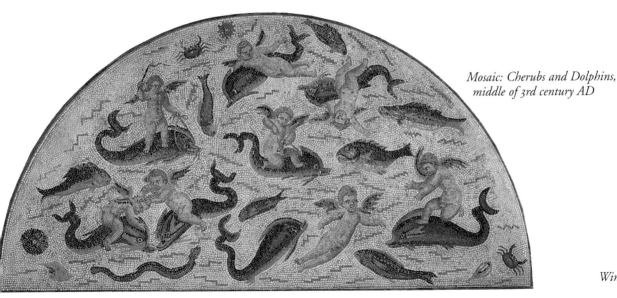

*Mosaic: Cherubs and Dolphins,
middle of 3rd century AD*

Cherubs and Dolphins

Chubby-cheeked cherubs riding on dolphins are racing through a sea full of fish. This scene decorated a fountain in a lavish Roman abode in Africa. The technique of mosaic, which fits together little cubes of colored glass, enabled the artist to create stone pictures that come close to paintings.

*Winged Guardian,
c. 40-60 BC*

Winged Guardian

Roman houses were comfortable and attractive. The houses of Pompeii, Herculanum and Boscoreale were buried under the embers of Vesuvius in 79, and all their treasures were preserved for us to see. This winged guardian painted on a wall protected the entrance to a room in Fannius Synistor's home.

Like a Photo Album

A little boy is dead. His parents chose a stone coffin for him, decorated with sculptures that recount his childhood, from his mother's breast to school.

The First Christians

During the Roman era a new religion was born: Christianity. After the death of Jesus Christ, the apostles set off across the world spreading the word of the Gospel. Saint Paul went to Greece, Saint Peter went to Rome. Christianity spread across the whole of the Roman Empire and became its official religion at the end of the 4th century.

Christ and Abbot Mena, 7th century

Virgin Mary, end of the 5th century

A Golden Abbot

The Egyptian Christians, known as Copts, built and decorated monasteries. They created this painted wood panel for the monastery at Baouit, depicting Christ and the Abbot Mena, head of the order. It is one of the first icons.

Down came Angel Gabriel

Mary is spinning the wool lying in the basket. The angel Gabriel, whose leg alone remains visible, comes down to announce that she will be the mother of Jesus. She looks quite astonished. This delicate image was sculpted in fig wood by Egyptian Christians.

By the Grace of God

A Roman emperor prances on a horse while the vanquished people bring him the spoils of his victory. Christ blesses this scene of war, thereby giving the emperor divine power.

Barberini Ivory, first half of the 6th century

▶ Consecrated Wine

The floor of the church at Kabr Hiram in Lebanon was decorated with this mosaic. It includes scenes from hunting, wrestling and country life: a farmer's wife is chasing a fox, a shepherd is playing a flute, a peasant is leading his mule. In the middle are two wine-producers crushing grapes in a press.

Kabr Hiram Mosaic, middle of the 6th century

And Mohammed Created Islam

As Christianity developed, the prophet Mohammed established the foundations of a new religion: Islam. After his death in 632, his disciples, the Muslims, collected his lessons in the Koran and took up their arms. In one hundred years they conquered an enormous territory that stretched from Spain to India. In all the Muslim countries skillful craftsmen decorated the palaces and mosques with intricate patterns and designed beautiful objects.

Cup with Prince and Falcon, beginning of the 13th century

The Prince and the Falcon

This young man is a prince. He is leaving to hunt on his prancing horse. The moonlike face, almond eyes and tiny mouth correspond to the oriental ideal of beauty in the 13th century.

From Elephant to Parrot

This little ivory box belonged to one of the sons of the Kalif Abd Alrahman II, who reigned over an immense territory from his home in Spain. It was intricately sculpted in an elephant's tusk. Gazelles, lions and parrots fill the design with life.

Ivory Pyxis belonging to Al-Mughera, c. 968

◀ Scenes from Paradise

A man and a woman talking intimately in a garden, a lion roaring against the setting sun, flowers everywhere... these interlocking star-shaped scenes, sometimes bordered with a frieze of delicate inscriptions, are what remains of this decorative furnishing. They covered the walls of an Iranian vault.

Decorative Panel, 1267

The Scented Lion

A few drops of precious incense burnt in this openwork bronze lion would be enough to perfume a room.

Lion Incense Burner, 11th century

The Middle Ages

The Middle Ages traditionally cover one thousand years stretching from the fall of the Roman Empire (476) to the discovery of America by Christopher Columbus (1492).

Emperor Charlemagne

We cannot say with certainty whether this horseman with thick drooping mustaches is Charlemagne or his grandson, Charles the Bald, who tried to look like his grand-father. The statuette is made of bronze and is less than 25 cm tall. It draws its inspiration from Roman equestrian statues.

Equestrian Statuette of Charlemagne, 9th century

The Treasures of the Kings of France

The fabulous treasures of the Kings of France date back to the Middle Ages. They were enriched over the following centuries. Before coming to the Louvre, they were kept at the Saint-Denis Abbey. They include the precious objects or *regalia* used during the coronations.

Crown of Charlemagne, 1804

A Legendary Sword

According to the legend, this sword, known as the "Joyeuse," belonged to Charlemagne. But this is far from being certain. It was used in the coronation of the Kings of France.

Coronation Sword of the Kings of France, 10th-11th centuries

Guarded from on High

Charles V (1338-1380) had this gold scepter decorated with a statuette of his ancestor Charlemagne.

Charles V Scepter, 14th century

Let Justice be Done

This marvelous little ivory hand is the image of the absolute power that the Kings of France had in matters of justice. It bears the precious ring of Saint Denis.

Hand of Justice, beginning of the 13th century

Serpentine Paten, c. 875-900

Oh For the Glory of Charlemagne!

In 1804, Napoleon I had this crown made for his coronation. He pompously called it the *Crown of Charlemagne*, but only the cameos could have belonged to his illustrious predecessor.

Gold Fish

Little golden fish dart across the deep green background of this serpentine saucer. The surround is encrusted with emeralds, sapphires and garnets. King Charles II, the Bald (843-877), used it for the sacred host during mass.

Glory be to God

In the Middle Ages all art was religious. At the beginning of the 11th century the bishops initiated many major projects. They asked craftsmen to carve scenes from the Bible and from the life of Jesus to decorate the churches. For the people of this period, most of whom did not know how to read or write, the churches became giant picture books. These stone sculptures are known as "Romanesque" art, which is recognizable by its geometrical patterns, static figures and imaginary creatures.

A Gigantic Christ

The crucifixion was one of the most popular subjects amongst artists. This one is wooden and was once painted in colors. Carved at the beginning of the 12th century in Burgundy, it was part of a group which probably included Saint John and the Virgin Mary.

Descent from the Cross, wood, c. 1125-1150

Marble Capital, end of the 11th century

Miracle in the Lions' Den

The prophet Daniel was thrown to the lions, but miraculously survived. On this upper segment, or capital, from one of the columns of the church of Sainte-Geneviève in Paris, Daniel stares dreamily out from between two impassive monsters.

Our Lady of Baroilles, stone, beginning of the 13th century

Clear Colors for the Virgin Mary

Sitting up straight on her throne, the baby Jesus on her knee, Our Lady of Baroilles has preserved her original bright colors.

Under the Angel's ▶ Instructions

The Apostle Matthew, here represented as a young man, is writing out the Epistle as the angel dictates it. This low relief sculpture has a charming natural look evoking everyday life.

At the beginning of the 13th century, religious art began to evolve into the "Gothic" style, which is freer and more elegant. The sculptures became more animated, and the artists strove to achieve a formal harmony. In Paris, the Sainte-Chapelle and the part of Notre-Dame begun under Saint Louis (1214-1270) illustrate this development.

The Saint Strikes the Devil

St. Michael's lance has disappeared with passage of time, but his vigorous assault remains clear. With a calm expression he is running his weapon through the devil cowering at his feet. His youthful, angelic face contrasts sharply with the devil's tormented look.

The Angel Dictating to St. Matthew the Evangelist, stone, c. 1250

St. Michael Striking Down the Devil, c. 1425

Virgin and Child from the Sainte-Chapelle, ivory, c. 1250-1260

Mary's Smile

This ivory statuette was carved in the 13th century in a large elephant's tusk. The artist has surpassed himself in reproducing the elegant folds of her gown and the delicate features of her face as faithfully as possible.

Faces

From the middle of the 14th century, the important members of society took to having their portrait painted by artists. They chose to be portrayed as they were in reality, in miniature and large-scale paintings. The novelty in this stemmed from the fact that they were represented alone, and not in groups kneeling beside the Virgin Mary and the baby Jesus.

John the Good

This is the first "independent" portrait known to us. This man, shown in profile with a slight smile on his lips, against a gold background, is John II, the Good, who reigned in France from 1350 to 1364. The name of the painter has been lost in the mists of time.

Portrait of John the Good, wood, panel before 1350

Jean Hey, Dauphin Charles-Orlant, 1494

Jean Fouquet, Self-Signed Portrait, c. 1450

Jean Fouquet

The painter pictured himself on a enamel medallion which was set into the frame of a two paneled painting called a diptych.

◄ Charles V and Jeanne of Bourbon

Charles V was the son of John the Good. He reigned from 1364 to 1380, during which time he transformed the Louvre fortress into a palace. This statue and the one of his wife decorated one of the portals. The sculptor gave a faithful reproduction of their features.

Charles V, King of France, and Jeanne of Bourbon, end of the 14th century

Charles VII

Charles VII was crowned by Jeanne d'Arc at Rheims in 1429. He was an unfortunate looking man. To disguise this fact, Fouquet concentrated on his royal garment with its padded shoulders.

Charles-Orlant

This little boy is the Dauphin Charles-Orlant, who would have become King if he had not died at the age of three. Anne of Brittany had this portrait painted to send to Charles VII, the boy's father, who had gone to war.

Jean Fouquet, Portrait of Charles VII, c. 1445-1450

Chilling!

Towards the end of the Middle Ages, vaults became elaborate monuments. The corpse was represented lying down in its real size, fixed in stone forever. Certain people commissioned even more imposing monuments during their lifetime. This is the monumental and decidedly macabre scene that the powerful seneschal Philippe Pot dreamed up so that he would never be forgotten.

A Mournful Procession

Eight mourners, their faces hidden under heavy hoods, are carrying their lord to his grave. They are made of painted stone. Each one is holding an emblazoned shield. The eight different coats of arms prove that his nobility stretches back at least eight generations.

Tomb of Philippe Pot,
last quarter of the 15th century

All Change in Italy

While artists in France were busy sculpting, in Italy they were painting. At the end of the 13th century a painter called Giotto invented a new way of painting. He represented real landscapes and gave his figures expressive faces. This marked the end of Byzantine art, which had dominated the Mediterranean for over 1000 years. It was the end of paintings of impassive and stiff figures shown against gold backgrounds.

Columns of Angels

Cimabue was Giotto's master. He was still close to Byzantium painters, who used art to celebrate God. On this large painting, which is more than 4 meters tall, the angels form two columns on either side of a majestical Virgin Mary. It has the traditional gold background.

Cimabue, Maestà.
The Madonna and Child in Majesty
Surrounded by Angels, c. 1270

The Byzantine Model

This medallion showing Saint Demetrios is an example of a Byzantine icon. Prayers were said before this sacred object.

St. Demetrios,
gold and enamel,
beginning of the 12th century

The Saint Who Spoke to the Birds

This scene shows St. Francis of Assisi talking to the birds. It is a detail from a large painting executed on the altarpiece of the church at Pisa. Giotto gave free reign to his sensibility. His image of the saint is human and familiar.

Giotto,
St. Francis of Assisi, c. 1295-1300
Detail : the saint speaks to the birds.

The Renaissance

The Extraordinary Italian Flowering

All eyes on Italy! The 15th century was a truly revolutionary time. It has been likened to a second birth or "naissance," hence the term "Re-naissance." Painters, sculptors and architects rediscovered classical art and used it to invent new forms. They tried to represent depth and volume, as well as learning to use light and shade. They looked at man and nature with a fresh eye. Florence, the city of the Medicis royalty, became the capital of art, whose brilliance shone across all of Italy.

Gabriel and Mary
This wooden Madonna, painted in striking colors, is facing the archangel Gabriel and listening carefully to his news that she will soon give birth to the Messiah.

Domenico di Niccolo dei Chori, Archangel Gabriel, The Virgin of the Annunciation, c. 1420-1430

Fra Angelico, The Coronation of the Virgin, c. 1430

A Crown for the Madonna
Fra Angelico, the monk who loved painting, has used his delicate brushwork here to pick out the crowds of angels, saints and men of the church gathered around the throne to witness the coronation of the Virgin Mary. Each face is a true portrait.

The High-Headed Princess

The profile of this young girl, painted against a background of flowers and butterflies, is quite astonishing. Her hair has been pulled up under a small head-piece and probably removed from the front of her head to show the extent of her forehead, which was a sign of nobility and intelligence. The sprig of juniper embroidered on her shoulder is a symbol of peace and happiness.

Pisanello, Portrait of Ginevra d'Este, c. 1435

Portrait of a Tyrant

Piero della Francesca has played subtly with light and shadow to shape the facial contours of Sigismondo Malatesta, the tyrant who brought terror to his city of Rimini. It was thought for a long time that his wife was the high-headed princess to his left.

Piero della Francesca, Portrait of Sigismondo Malatesta, c. 1430

A Relief Painting

The famous architect and painter, Donatello, modeled this Madonna in clay before painting it and adding gold plate. The result is a chef d'oeuvre of painting and sculpture. Mary's face is troubled as if she knew that a great and tragic fate awaited her child.

Donatello, Virgin and Child, c. 1440

A New Way of Painting

During the first half of the 15th century, when France was just beginning to recover from the Hundred Years War, painters all over Europe were questioning their art. The Italian Paolo Uccello was passionate about perspective. He tried all sorts of ways of painting in three dimensions, even losing sleep over it! At the same time, in Holland, the Van Eyck brothers discovered - or rediscovered - oil painting. Prior to this time, painters had used egg white to bind their colors. Oil differs from egg white in that it takes longer to dry, allowing the painter to touch up his work without leaving a brush mark.

Paolo Uccello,
The Battle of San Romano,
c. 1455

Rhythm and Movement

On this large panel, which is over 3 meters long, Uccello has painted a scene from the Battle of San Romano, which took place in 1432 between the people of Florence and those of Siena. If you look along the painting from right to left, the horses' hooves start to gallop and the lances fly... It comes alive! The forest of legs in the middle distance is suggestive of depth.

The World in a Painting

The man kneeling before the Virgin Mary is Nicolas Rolin, a high dignitary in the court of Philippe the Good, duke of Burgundy. He commissioned this little painting from Van Eyck. The painter portrayed the people with extraordinary realism, capturing all the minute details. The landscape in the background is a masterly miniature carefull worth scrutiny.

Jan Van Eyck,
The Madonna of
Chancellor Rolin,
c 1434

Heavenly Creatures and Earthly Souls

In the 15th century it was no longer only the Church that commissioned art. The works created for princes and wealthy families enabled painters to explore subjects other than religious imagery. They were drawn to all aspects of human life and rediscovered mythology.

Tears of Blood

Giovanni Bellini came from an illustrious family of painters. He depicted Christ as a pale man who has suffered terribly, but is still full of kindness when he gives his benediction to mankind after the Resurrection.

Giovanni Bellini,
Christ's Blessing,
c. 1470

◄ Nose to Nose

The man with the strangely puffy nose is hardly beautiful. But he is looking at the blond boy with such gentleness! Is this a grand-father with his grandson, one at the dawn of his life, the other in his twilight years?

Ghirlandaio,
The Old Man and the Young Boy, c. 1490

A Bouquet of Young Girls

There is no equal to the Florentine Botticelli for capturing the grace of young girls. This fresco painted on the wall of a Florentine villa shows a young fiancée receiving gifts from Venus, goddess of beauty, who is accompanied by the three Graces.

Botticelli, Venus and the Graces
Offering Gifts to a Young Girl, c. 1480

François I
and the Others:
Family Portraits

During the reign of François I, in the 16th century, it became fashionable to have a realistic portrait painted, generally a bust turned at an angle or in full frontal, against a neutral background. The King's official painter, Jean Clouet, his son François and Corneille de Lyon, a Dutchman living in France, all carried out detailed portraits in which the face and dress are reproduced with great accuracy. François I's descendants continued to commission their portraits.

Jean Clouet,
Portrait of
François I,
c. 1530

Henri II
Son of François I, he married the great Catherine of Médicis and reigned over France for 23 years.

Workshop of
François Clouet,
Portrait of
Henri II,
King from
1547-1559

François I
François I, known as a seducer and friend of the arts, is depicted here with a slight smile, wearing a splendid Italian-style jacket.

Anonymous, Portrait of
Catherine of Médicis,
Queen from 1547 to 1589

Catherine of Médicis
For 35 years, until her death in 1589, she reigned obscurely over a disorganized France. Three of her sons were to become King, but Henri IV declared her to be the truly great King!

A Lord
*Workshop of
Corneille de Lyon,
Jean d'Albon,
Lord of Saint-André, c. 1550*

Charles IX
Son of Henri II. He is sadly notorious for having ordered the Massacre on Saint-Bartholomew's day, the 24th of August 1572, when thousands of Protestants were killed. He died soon after, at the age of 24.

Workshop of François Clouet, Portrait of Charles IX, King from 1560-1574

Elisabeth of Austria
This young Austrian married King Charles IX, but was widowed at the age of 20 and returned to finish her days in her homeland.

*François Clouet,
Elisabeth of Austria,
Queen from 1560-1592*

A Young Man
*Corneille de Lyon,
Young Man*

A Noble Lady
*Workshop of François Clouet,
Claude de Beaune de Semblançay,
dame de Chateaubrun, c. 1520*

The Chemist
Serious and stiff in his dark robes, the apothecary Pierre Quthe is shown beside his herbal.

*François Clouet,
Pierre Quthe,
Apothecary, 1562*

Clément Marot
*Corneille de Lyon,
Clément Marot, c. 1530.*
He was François I's favorite poet.

Four Italian Geniuses

Raphael, Titian and Michelangelo, Leonardo da Vinci... four true geniuses! The 16th century got off to a good start in Italy. Renaissance art reached its pinnacle. Their compositions have the harmony and simplicity that makes them perfect masterpieces. François I was a great admirer of Italian painting and he brought Leonardo da Vinci to his court in 1516, beginning a sumptuous collection of paintings and sculptures by the Italian Masters.

Raphael,
Balthazar Castiglione,
c. 1514-1515

Titian,
Concert champêtre,
c. 1550

The Wise Balthazar

Balthazar Castiglione, both a diplomat and a writer, was also a friend of Raphael. Beyond the physical resemblance, the painter has captured his model's personality, his measured and humane nature. The clear gaze combined with the harmonious range of blacks, grays and beiges show his quiet confidence.

Musical Beauties

Titian was just twenty years old when he painted this country scene. Why are the two women naked? Are they muses? The soft golden light of a summer evening gives this scene a calm and tranquil aspect.

Rising Out of the Marble

This slave, over 2 meters heigh, was intended as one of several figures for the mausoleum of Pope Julius II. But Michelangelo changed his project and this statue remained unfinished.

Michelangelo,
Slave Dying,
marble, 1513-1515

Leonardo da Vinci,
La Gioconda, 1501-1506

Mona Lisa's Smile

This painting has become the very emblem of the Louvre. Leonardo da Vinci himself was very attached to this portrait, and he never gave it away. It is said that this young woman had just lost her daughter. To cheer her up the painter called in some acrobats, which is why she is smiling somewhat sadly.

Immense
or Minuscule

At 10 meters by 6, one of these paintings is the biggest painting in the Louvre. The other one is no bigger than 21 centimeters by 18, and it is one of the smallest. Both were painted during the same period, in the second half of the 16th century. One comes from the south of Europe, the other from the North, and the painters were certainly unknown to one another. Paolo Veronese was a flamboyant Venetian who specialized in decorative painting. Pieter Brueghel was Flemish and his work is dense and mysterious. They represent the extremes of luxury and misery!

5 Lame Beggars

*Pieter Brueghel,
The Beggars,
1568*

Brueghel has painted the sort of cripples who peopled church doorsteps in an era when surgeons didn't hesitate to amputate limbs. Was Brueghel's intention to satirize the four classes of society represented by the king, the bishop, the soldier and the peasant, who are recognizable by their hats?

130 guests at the Wedding

The monks of San Giorgio Maggiore commissioned this episode of the life of Christ from Veronese to decorate the walls of their refectory. It depicts

the Wedding Feast at Cana, when Jesus performed his first miracle by changing water into wine. This biblical scene is treated with all the splendor of a Venetian banquet.

Veronese,
The Wedding Feast at Cana,
1562-1563

Far North

There is no denying it, Northern painters do not paint like those in the South! They have a penchant for stories, and they like to depict domestic scenes in all their detail. Like the Italian painters, they also experienced a Renaissance, but it came slightly later, at the beginning of the 16th century when the religious reform that led to Protestantism was in full swing. Since religious images had become somewhat suspicious, painters turned their attention to human life.

Thorny Portrait

This self-portrait by Albrecht Dürer was probably painted for his fiancée. The thistle he is holding is a sign of fidelity. Dürer was the first painter to execute a portrait expressing his subject's feelings and character.

Albrecht Dürer, Self-Portrait, 1493

front

A Mad Escapade

A few drunkards, a clown, a nun and a monk are setting off to the land of Folly. Hieronymus Bosch knew just how to play on popular beliefs and fear, mixing fantasy and realism. This little painting - 58 by 22 centimeters - is the only work of his in the Louvre.

Hieronymus Bosch, The Ship of Fools, c. 1500

Clad in Hair Alone

Mary Magdalene, the sinful saint who is clad only in her hair, has always been a popular subject for artists. Here Gregor Erhart has almost certainly drawn inspiration from a Dürer etching for his life-size limewood statue.

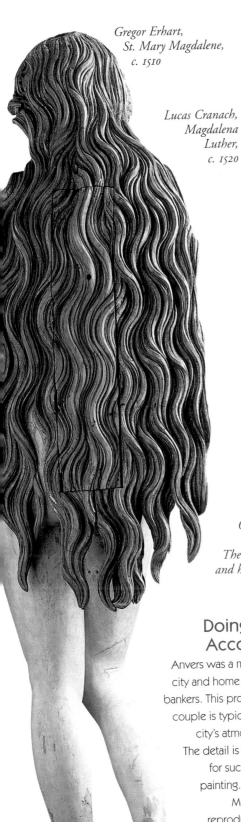

Gregor Erhart,
St. Mary Magdalene,
c. 1510

Lucas Cranach,
Magdalena
Luther,
c. 1520

Her Father Transformed History

This pale little girl with long blond hair is probably Magdalena Luther, daughter of Martin Luther who founded Protestantism. Lucas Cranach was a well-known painter in Germany and one of Dürer's pupils.

A Penny for Her Thoughts

The portrait of this woman is wonderfully delicate, with soft, refined colors. It was done by Hans Memling, the greatest painter from Bruges.

Hans Memling,
Portrait of
an Old Woman,
c. 1480

Quentin
Metsys,
The Banker
and his Wife,
c. 1514

Doing the Accounts

Anvers was a merchant city and home to many bankers. This prosperous couple is typical of the city's atmosphere. The detail is amazing for such a small painting. Quentin Metsys has reproduced the gold pieces, pearls, illuminated book, scales and mirror with great accuracy.

back

Henri IV, King of Peace

At the end of the 16th century the Wars of Religion between Catholics and Protestants had transformed France into a bloody battleground. When he came to the throne in 1589, Henri IV brought peace because he was himself a Protestant converted to Catholicism. With the help of his faithful minister, Sully, he launched a new era of prosperity. He made Paris into a modern capital and encouraged artistic creation by bringing artists from Northern Protestant countries and Italy. He was assassinated by Ravaillac in 1610.

*Pierre Biard,
Fame, 1597*

Sound the Trumpets!

The woman blowing the trumpet is announcing the king's great repute. Her body seems to fly through the air. This statue exemplifies the Mannerist style that was popular in France and Italy at this time.

Renaissance Beauties

Henri IV's lovely mistress, Gabrielle d'Estrées, bore him a son. Her sister pinching her breast evokes her motherhood and the ring held in her left hand symbolizes her secret relation with the king. The bodies of the two women are white and smooth, their posture and gestures refined.

*Anonymous,
Gabrielle d'Estrées
and one of her Sisters,
c. 1594*

The King Has No Clothes On

Inspired by the gods of Antiquity, the king and queen chose to have themselves represented as Jupiter and Juno, almost entirely naked. It took some daring! Prieur, who was the greatest sculptor during the reign of Henri IV, earned himself a fortune selling his busts of the royal couple.

*Barthélémy Prieur,
Henri IV as Jupiter
and Marie of Médicis
as Juno, 1600-1610*

Massacres Through the Ages

The painter Caron wanted to depict the massacre of the Huguenots before the arrival of Henri IV on the throne. To do so subtly, he used a scene from ancient history as a pretext. The picture shows the massacres ordered by Mark Antony, Octavian and Lepidus in first-century BC Rome.

*Antoine Caron, The Massacres
of the Triumvirate, 1566*

The Triumphant 17th century

Inventions Galore!

In 1610, when his father Henri IV died, Louis XIII was only 9 years old. Later, with the help of Richelieu, he re-established order in France. Paris became the capital of the arts, a modern city where artists flourished.

The King

Richelieu, the powerful prime minister, commissioned this portrait of Louis XIII to decorate the "gallery of illustrious men" in his palace. Naturally, he called on the greatest portrait artist of the period, Philippe de Champaigne.

Philippe de Champaigne, detail of Louis XIII crowned by Victory, 1635

Georges de La Tour, The Trickster with the Ace of Diamonds, c. 1630

Secret Senses

Protestant painters brought still-life painting back into fashion because they refused to paint religious or frivolous scenes. The objects here represent each of the five senses: the lute is hearing, the flowers are smell, the chess board is touch, the mirror is sight and the bread is taste.

Lubin Baugin (c. 1612-1663)
Still Life with Chess Board

Trickery

The rather naive young man in this painting is surely going to lose the gold pieces lying in front of him. A crafty-looking trickster has drawn an ace of diamonds out of his pocket to ensure his victory. With this lavish play of hands, eyes and colors, La Tour has given us one of the finest card tricks in history.

Out of the King's Eye

It was quite unprecedented to depict peasants in their home environment. The Le Nain brothers often used these modest subjects, who were neither Kings nor wealthy nobles, as models. The colors here evoke the soil of Lorraine where they labored.

Louis or Antoine Le Nain,
The Peasant Family, 1642

Too Much!

There was nothing peaceful about the beginning of the 17th century. It was all excess. Artists gave themselves up entirely to their overflowing imagination. Filled with ardor, they painted with large brush-strokes, making their clouds swirl, their figures spin and their colors clash to produce contrasts of light and shade. One Italian painter, Caravaggio, showed real originality. His style was so extraordinary that it came to be known as Caravaggiesque style. Other great masters flourished with these new and freer forms. It was known as Baroque art, after the Italian word "barocco," which means an irregular pearl.

A Flemish Weddings ▶

After her husband, Henri IV, died, Marie of Médicis became regent. She requested Rubens, the great Flemish master, to recount her life in 24 huge paintings. In this scene her portrait is presented to her future husband. Jupiter and Juno are looking tenderly over the couple. Drapery and clouds billow around them and the figures are restless. This is art at its most Baroque.

Pierre Paul Rubens,
Henri IV Receives the Portrait of
Marie de Médicis, 1622-1625

Caravaggio,
Death of the Virgin,
c. 1605-1606

A Roman Death

The Italian painter Caravaggio was a true revolutionary. No-one would have dared depict the Madonna as an ordinary dead woman, with swollen feet and stomach. His model had drowned in the Tiber. Many artists followed his example, especially in the technique of contrasting patches of light and shade.

From Rome to London, Artists Took to the Road

It was part of the traditional education of an artist to spend a period of time abroad. Sometimes they also chose to remain there. During the Renaissance, Italian painters came to France. In the 17th century it was the turn of French painters to go to Italy. Flemish and Dutch artists, on the other hand, were drawn to England.

A Frenchman in Rome

This picture was painted by the great Nicolas Poussin. He went to Rome to study and liked it so much that he stayed. Here he has depicted the biblical scene of the Judgment of Solomon. Two women are arguing over a baby. Pretending to be just, Solomon orders that each woman should have half the child. One accepts and the other refuses this terrible judgment: the latter is the true mother and Solomon gives her the child.

Nicolas Poussin,
The Judgment of Solomon, 1649

A Much-Copied Italian Master

Numerous foreign artists came to Bologna to see the Italian painter Guido Reni. They copied his lively compositions, drawing inspiration from his striking colors. Here Reni has painted the mythological scene in which Helen is carried off by the shepherd Paris.

Guido Reni,
The Abduction of Helen, 1626-1629

A Dutchman in London

Here is the King of England, Charles I, brother-in-law of Louis XIII, getting ready for the hunt. His favorite painter was the Dutchman Van Dyck. He has depicted the King in a casual pose, without crown or mantle.

Anton Van Dyck,
Charles I at the Hunt, 1635

Hopelessly in Love with Italy

This dazzling yellow evokes gold, and the woman dressed in it symbolizes wealth. Like Poussin, Simon Vouet would have loved to stay in Rome, but Louis XIII called him back to Paris.

Simon Vouet,
Allegory of Wealth, 1640

The Sun King

Who was the greatest, most magnificent and most triumphant King of France? Louis XIV, of course! He commissioned innumerable palaces, monuments, sculptures and paintings throughout his reign, which lasted a full 72 years, from the age of 5 to 77. He was lord of everything, including the arts. No monarch before him had done so much to secure his reputation.

François Girardon, Louis XIV on Horseback, 1692

Dressed as a Roman Emperor

In the garb of a Roman Emperor, but with a curled wig, Louis XIV is riding out majestically. This equestrian statue by Girardon is the small-scale model of an imposing statue that is now lost.

Oh To Be Alexander the Great!

Charles Le Brun was the greatest artist of Louis XIV's reign. By depicting the victories of Alexander the Great, who was never defeated, his intention was to glorify Louis XIV, who was also always triumphant.

Charles Le Brun, Alexander in Babylon, 1660-1665

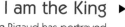

I am the King ▶

Here Rigaud has portrayed the King with all the trappings of royalty: the ermine gown, the scepter and the crown. At 63, Louis XIV is at his most magnificent. He had intended to send this portrait to his grandson, the King of Spain, but he liked it so much that he decided to keep it.

Hyacinthe Rigaud, Portrait of Louis XIV, 1701

The Great Era of a Great King

The era of Louis XIV is generally considered to have been a golden age in France because his reign was so long and brilliant. Louis XIV insisted that all artistic creation should be to his glory. He entrusted Colbert with royal commissions and relied on the painter Le Brun to give direction to other artists. He enlarged and decorated his palace at Versailles, as well as fitting out several smaller palaces, like Marly, where he retreated for some rest from the lavish life of the court.

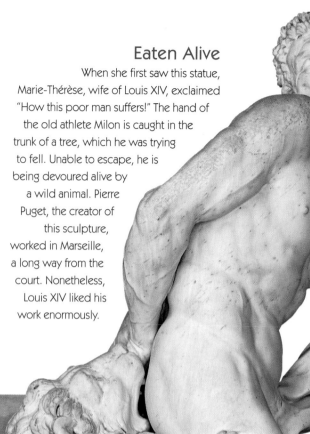

Eaten Alive

When she first saw this statue, Marie-Thérèse, wife of Louis XIV, exclaimed "How this poor man suffers!" The hand of the old athlete Milon is caught in the trunk of a tree, which he was trying to fell. Unable to escape, he is being devoured alive by a wild animal. Pierre Puget, the creator of this sculpture, worked in Marseille, a long way from the court. Nonetheless, Louis XIV liked his work enormously.

A Majestic Minister

When one is second only to the king, one's portrait must be fittingly regal and executed by the best painter in the kingdom. The Chancellor Séguier chose to pose on a superb horse, dressed in sumptuous robes and surrounded by all number of valets who are there to escort him and protect him with peculiar little umbrellas.

Charles Le Brun,
The Chancellor
Séguier, c. 1657-1661

Pierre Puget,
Milon of Croton,
1670-1683

Never too Beautiful for a King

The King's palaces were exquisitely decorated. The two magnificent bouquets on the doors of this wardrobe, made by the cabinetmaker Boulle for the King, are composed of brass, pewter and colored woods against a tortoiseshell background.

André-Charles-Boulle, Wardrobe, around 1700

The King's Gardens

Louis XIV had a passion for gardens. He had the one at Versailles designed by a truly great gardener called Le Nôtre, who created exquisite vistas. He also ordered numerous statues to enliven the beds, ponds and groves. The King was so pleased with the results that he wrote a little guide entitled quite simply, "How to Display Gardens."

Guillaume Coustou,
Horse Restrained
by a Groom,
1739-1745

Glorious Horses

Louis XIV loved to retreat to Marly, a small palace located near Versailles. He had the gardens decorated with many statues. A pair of winged horses dominated the horse-pond, one mounted by Fame, blowing into her trumpet, the other by Mercury, the messenger of the gods. Louis XV was also very fond of Marly. He replaced the statues commissioned by his great grandfather with two superb horses pulling against the restraining movement of vigorous grooms. All of these statues are now to be found in the Louvre, where they are protected from air pollution.

Antoine Coysevox,
Mercury Riding
Pegasus,
1698-1702

The Golden Age

While France was enjoying its Great Epoch, the Spanish, Flemish and Dutch were certainly not missing out on the golden age. Having been overshadowed for a long time by France and Italy, they now came into their own. Great artists, such as Rembrandt, Vélazquez, and Vermeer, painted stunning masterpieces. From intimate scenes of home life in Flanders to great portraits of the Spanish court, diversity was the order of the day.

The Beggar

This young beggar is probably picking out his fleas. Murillo painted several pictures of street children.

Bartolomé Esteban Murillo, The Young Beggar, c. 1650

Ow!

There was no alternative – dentists in the 17th century pulled their patients' teeth without any anesthetic! The man's clenched fists indicate his unbearable pain. The Dutchman Gerard Dou showed an exceptional talent for depicting everyday scenes.

Gerard Dou, The Dentist, 1647

The Spanish Fiancée

To secure peace between France and Spain, the young Louis XIV had to marry a Spanish princess. The wedding took place in 1661. The young girl was called Marie-Thérèse. Vélazquez, the greatest Spanish painter of his time, painted her portrait.

Johannes Vermeer, The Lacemaker, c. 1665-1670

Workshop of Diego Vélazquez, The Young Marie-Thérèse (1638-1683), c. 1661

Mysterious Northern Lights

In the translucent atmosphere of her room, a young girl bends over her delicate lacework. The peace is undisturbed. Not even the buzzing of a fly. The light harmonizes the different colors, creating the mystery that makes Vermeer's art so compelling.

Contrasted 18th Century

*Edme Bouchardon,
Cupid Making
a Bow from the Mace
of Hercules,
1750*

Naughty!

In the 18th century, a playful spirit got hold of painting. Watteau, Fragonard and Boucher undertook to depict a certain way of life in France, a mixture of pleasure, gallantry and devilishness. It was quite a party!

The Nude Goddess

Mythology is a bare pretext here for the artist to show two naked young girls in a natural setting. But appearances are maintained: a bow, some arrows and a decent hunting picture are there to indicate that this is Diana, the Huntress.

*François Boucher,
Diana out of the Bath, 1742*

Love, love, love...

Bouchardon made endless preparatory sketches for this royal commission. He even took a cast of his model's arms and legs so that his Cupid would be most life-like. But this was precisely what his public didn't like: his Cupid was not round and dimpled enough.

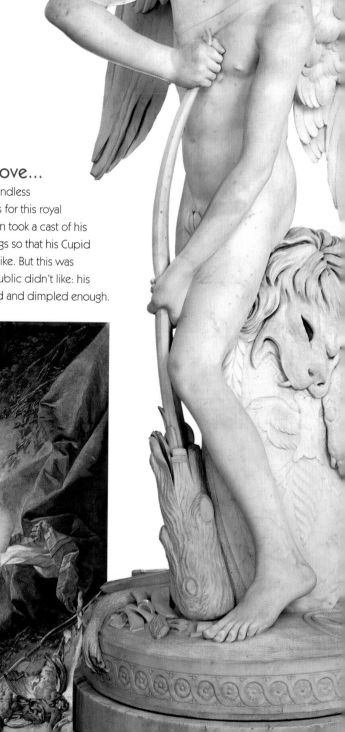

Jean-Honoré Fragonard,
The Bolt, 1776-79

In the bedroom...

The ardent young man is
pushing home the bolt. The
young girl is trying gently to
stop him, and her "no" sounds
suspiciously like a "yes." The
apple on the table evokes the
first scene of temptation when
Eve ate the forbidden apple.

Meanwhile
in Italy...

Tiepolo has captured
the spirit of the
Venice carnival. Out
of the crowd comes
the Italian Punchinello
with his long nose
and huge white hat.

Giandomenico Tiepolo,
Carnival Scene,
c. 1754-55

79

The Famous and the Forgettable

What do the Marquise of Pompadour and a comic Pierrot have in common? Or Voltaire, Diderot and Madame de Tronchin? Not much is the answer, except for the fact that they lived at the same time and were painted in the inimitable eighteenth-century way. Today, on the walls of the Louvre, they share the same glory. The unknown figures of yesterday are just as unforgettable.

Chardin as seen by Chardin

Chardin was 72 years old when he drew this pastel portrait. He depicted himself as he saw himself, in his nightgown, with a scarf around his neck and a nightcap on his head.

Chardin, Self-Portrait, 1771

Sad Clown

Watteau was a great fan of Italian comic theater and he painted this life-size Pierrot the Clown. With his hands hanging limply against his white satin costume, Pierrot seems to be wondering what he is doing there, in the middle of the canvas. In the background four other comic characters are involved in a mysterious discussion.

Jean-Antoine Watteau, Pierrot, 1718

Mme de Pompadour, the King's Beloved.

This pastel is more than 1.7 meters high, and it shows Mme de Pompadour, the apple of Louis XV's eye. La Tour spent three years on this picture.

Maurice Quentin de La Tour, Portrait of the Marquise of Pompadour, c. 1755

Madame Tronchin

Madame Tronchin was Swiss, as was the artist Liotard who executed this delicate pastel. From under her vast cap, the 72 year old woman is giving us an enigmatic smile.

Jean-Étienne Liotard,
Portrait of Madame Jean Tronchin, 1758

Jean-Honoré Fragonard,
Diderot, 1760

Hello Mr. Diderot!

A sparkle in his eye, flowing hair and an easy posture - that is how Fragonard chose to depict the author of the Encyclopedia. There is nothing stiff or conventional in this portrait, which gives it the feeling of a sketch. A free-flowing homage to a free thinker!

Voltaire in the Flesh

The Greeks and Romans used to represent their heroes naked. The sculptor Pigalle wanted to revive this tradition by modeling the famous philosopher in the nude. But the bodies of the Ancients were muscular and strong, while Voltaire's is bony and a bit flabby. He was already an old man. Never mind. It was Voltaire's mind and not his body that made him heroic!

Jean-Baptiste Pigalle,
Voltaire, 1776

Sir Joshua
Reynolds,
Master Hare,
1788

Meanwhile in Great Britain...

Reynolds painted this portrait of little Francis Hare in 1788. Oh yes, this adorable little girl in a pink dress is... a boy! It was a time when little boys often had long hair and wore dresses.

Everyday Life

This was still a period when large religious and mythological scenes were highly popular, but artists also began to specialize in still lifes and intimate scenes called genre scenes. Chardin had such success with *The Skate* that Louis XV bought several paintings from him.

The Ghostly Skate

Chardin drew his inspiration from Flemish painting, especially for his combination of alive and dead animals. The arch-backed cat is already quite extraordinary. But it is the pallid skate, dripping with blood, that transfixes the viewer, just like a ghostly apparition.

Jean-Siméon Chardin,
The Skate, 1725

A Well-Groomed Child

With his immaculate wig and embroidered jacket, this young boy is looking unwaveringly at the spinning top. Chardin is without parallel for his ability to catch moments such as these, when time seems suspended.

Jean-Siméon
Chardin,
The Child and
the Spinning Top,
c. 1738

Fresh from ▶ the Farm

A basket of eggs, a freshly picked mushroom, two apples and a handful of chestnuts - this simple painting, which measures 38 by 48 cm, was received like a little gem in the year of 1789, when History was turned upside down by the Revolution.

Henri Horace Roland Delaporte,
The Basket of Eggs, 1788

A Family Snap under Louis XV

It is breakfast or tea time. Hot chocolate will be
served and the children will play with their toys.
It was almost certainly his own family that the painter
Boucher depicted in his beautiful Parisian apartment.

François Boucher,
Breakfast Time, 1739

Luis Eugenio Melendez,
Still Life with Figs,
c. 1760-1770

Meanwhile
in Spain...

Melendez painted
very realistic still lifes
in which the objects
seem to be lit by a
bright projector.

Revolutionary Undercurrents

At the end of the 18th century all sorts of artistic styles were practiced. Some painters produced frivolous or tender scenes, while others preferred more serious subjects. The Roman Empire was fashionable again. Was this perhaps a sign of the approaching turmoil? French society was in total upheaval, and in 1789 the Revolution destroyed the old order. The revolutionaries overturned the monarchy and executed King Louis XVI.

Jacques-Louis David, The Oath of the Horatii, 1784

Victory or Death ▶

The painter David had great sympathy for the Revolution. He painted the three legendary Horatii brothers just as they were swearing to their father that they would die rather than live under enemy rule. This scene from Roman mythology is a good illustration of the Revolutionary ideal.

Love Forever

Eros is waking up the sleeping nymph Psyche with a tender kiss. This sculpture is so ethereal that it seems to have been carved by the hand of a god. Canova dominated artistic life in Rome. He did a lot of work for Napoleon I and his family.

Antonio Canova, Eros and Psyche, 1793

She is the New Republic

This opulent woman who is unveiling the Declaration of the Rights of Man is Republic personified. As a good revolutionary, the painter Chinard paid his due to the new government.

Joseph Chinard, Republica, 1794

Motherly Love

Madame Vigée le Brun was Marie-Antoinette's favorite painter. Here she has portrayed herself with her daughter in her arms. She is dressed in "Grecian" style, as fashion dictated then, and her hair is gathered up like that of Greek statues.

Mme Vigée le Brun,
Self-Portrait with Daughter, 1789

The Lady with the Rose

Her dress is dark, her face is serious. A large pink flower in her hair is the only luxury this grand lady has allowed herself. She was already ill and she died soon after. Goya was the most fashionable portrait artist of his time, as well as being the King's official painter.

Goya, Portrait of the Countess del Carpio,
Marquise of Solona, c. 1792-1793

All Change in the 19th Century

*Antoine-Jean Gros,
Napoleon Bonaparte
on the Bridge at
Arcola, 1796*

Caught in Action

No other artist captured the
Napoleonic legend better
than Gros. Here he has
portrayed young general
Bonaparte attacking 40 000
Austrians in November 1796.
With a flag in one hand he is
sending his troops to do
battle on the bridge at
Arcola.

From Boyhood in Corsica...

The French Revolution was a bloody affair.
The French people needed to regain
confidence. Where was the hero to save them?
He appeared in the person of Napoleon
Bonaparte, general at the age of 22. Fifteen
years after the Revolution began, he was
named emperor under the title of Napoleon I.
His Empire only lasted 11 years: from 1804
to the final watershed at Waterloo in 1815.
But these few years were enough to project
the image of a new France across the world.
Napoleon brought back many treasures from
his conquests, which temporarily enriched
the Louvre collection, but most were returned
in 1815.

Imperial Vision

There are more than 100 figures in this painting of Napoleon and his wife Josephine's consecration. And they are all perfectly finished. David chose to depict the moment when the Emperor placed the crown on his wife's head. Napoleon was very pleased with it: "This is not a painting. You can stroll around in it." When looking at it from the right, the viewer does have the impression of being part of the crowd. David was impressed by Bonaparte's personality. He saw him as a hero in the style of ancient Roman generals. He accepted to serve his hero by becoming the official painter of the Empire.

Jacques Louis David,
The Consecration of the Emperor
Napoleon and the Coronation of
Empress Josephine, 1805-1808

... to Triumph as Emperor

Like Louis XIV

Gérard drew his inspiration from Rigaud's portrait of Louis XIV for this official representation of Napoleon. The Emperor has struck the same pose, standing in front of his throne under a large canopy. Copies of this painting were sent to all the provinces and conquered territories.

François Gérard,
Emperor Napoleon in his
Consecration Robes, 1805

Martin-Guillaume
Biennais, Tea Service made
for Napoleon I, 1810

War and Plagues

Gros has depicted Napoleon visiting the victims of the plague, which decimated his army. The future Emperor seems to be instilled with a miraculous power, as if he could cure these men with a simple gesture. Behind him an officer is holding his nose because of the plague-stricken people' smell.

Antoine Jean Gros,
Napoleon Bonaparte
Visiting the Plague Stricken
at Jaffa, 1804

◄ **Tea Please**

Napoleon commissioned this precious silver-gilt tea service just after his second marriage to Marie-Louise of Habsbourg in 1810. He had it decorated with eagles and bees, the new emblems that he had chosen to replace the *fleur-de-lys* of the Kings of France.

Incredible but Beautiful

In 1815 the Empire ended on a tragic note: the invincible Napoleon suffered defeat on defeat. Louis XVIII restored the monarchy, followed by his brother Charles X. France was once again ruled by kings. Unlike Napoleon, they didn't need art to glorify them, so artists were left increasingly to their own devices. The Restoration was a time when everything was possible and ambitions ran wild.

Ultra Fragile

A crystal chair could only be for a slight young woman like the Duchess of Berry. Her dressing table was also made of crystal. This unique work reveals extraordinary technical skill.

Crystal Dressing Table, 1819

Long in the Back

This lengthy back has more vertebrae than a normal back. Ingres certainly did this on purpose: with a shorter back this woman would have been quite ordinary. People criticized his lack of realism, but it is precisely what makes this nude so beautiful.

Ingres, Grande Odalisque, 1814

Catastrophe at Sea ▶

The frigate "Médusa" sunk off the coast of Africa. For 13 days 150 men drifted on a raft. Only 15 survived and were saved by a ship that saw them in the distance. They told of scenes of madness and cannibalism. Géricault studied real corpses in order to make his dead figures totally realistic.

Géricault, The Raft of the Medusa, 1819

The End of a World

Revolutions followed on revolutions: 1830, then 1848... The monarchy was finally put to rest, and the Republic began again... then it was the turn of the Second Empire. Artists gained greater freedom. They painted subjects that appealed to them... in particular the natural world.

The Simple Love of Nature

Corot painted this little picture in Italy, where he loved the light. He was one of the first painters to represent nature in and for itself, simply as it appeared to him. The Impressionists would later follow his example. They also worked with light, trying to capture the fleeting moment. Many of their paintings are shown in the Musée d'Orsay...

Jean-Baptiste Camille Corot, The Gardens of the Este Villa in Tivoli, 1843

The Long March to Freedom ▶

This woman wearing a revolutionary cap and brandishing the French flag high above her head is Liberty personified. As sparsely dressed as a Greek goddess, she is leading the people into the fray. She is a fictional apparition, but the corpses were quite real. Delacroix painted this picture shortly after the Revolution of 1830 which overturned Charles X. His successor, Louis-Philippe, liked it so much that he bought it!

Eugène Delacroix, Liberty Leading the People, 1830

Victory to the Strongest

Barye left nothing to chance in his attempt to capture the reality of this lion. He went every day to the Menagerie at the Jardins des Plantes in Paris to study the animals. The lion represents the King Louis-Philippe, who is doing away with his enemies, symbolized by the serpent.

Antoine-Louis Barye,
Lion Fighting
a Serpent, 1832-1835

800 Years of History

the court could take refuge in times of attack. But very quickly it came to be used as a prison. In 1214 Philippe-Auguste jailed Ferrand, the Count of Flanders, there, after he betrayed him during the Battle of Bouvines. This is the first historical reference to the Louvre. Today you can visit the foundations of the fortress and Louis-Auguste's moat. This is all that remains of the medieval Louvre.

The moats and ramparts

1189
BUILT
by Philippe-Auguste

King Philippe-August did not build the Louvre to live in, but rather as a fortress for Paris. The new castle had two draw-bridges, ramparts and deep moats. An enormous dungeon towered above the rest in the middle of the great rectangular courtyard, measuring more 30 meters in height. The Louvre was a stronghold, where

Around 1364-1369
TRANSFORMED
by Charles V

King Charles V decided to transform the imposing fortress into an elegant palace. He had windows opened up, a beautiful garden planted, and he commissioned wood paneling, sculpture and stained glass. When he took up abode there, the palace must have looked fine with its ten round towers reaching for the sky.

1528-1558
RENOVATED
by François I and Henri II

During the Renaissance, François I turned his attention to the Louvre, which was in great need of repair. He knocked down the dungeon and opened up the principal quadrangle. His son, Henri II, had a new wing built in the refined style of the period.

Gallery of the Cariatids, designed during the Renaissance

1595-1610
ENLARGED
by Henri IV

Henri IV had big ideas for his palace. He had a huge gallery, 500 meters long, built along the Seine to connect the old Louvre palace with the new Tuileries palace, begun by Catherine of Médicis, the widow of Henri II.

The Louvre under Charles V, detail from a 14th century painting

Henri IV's project for a greater Louvre

Napoleon I on the steps of the Louvre's new staircase

Around
1850-1870
"NAPOLEONIZED"

Napoleon III gave the Louvre the form that we know today. He practically doubled the palace's surface area, using it as a museum, an imperial residence and the seat of government. In 1871, during the week-long turmoil of the Commune, the rampaging Parisians set fire to the Tuileries palace, which was subsequently destroyed.

Napoleon III, detail from a painting by V.J. Chavet

Napoleon III's rooms

1981-2000
MODERNIZED
by François Mitterrand

The President of the Republic launched the "Grand Louvre" project, which was destined to last 20 years. The architect Ioeh Ming Peï designed the pyramid, which now marks the entrance to the Louvre. The old palace of the Kings of France has become the world's largest museum.

The Louvre today

1652-1665
EMBELLISHED
by Louis XIV

The Sun King wanted a Louvre worthy of his glory. He quadrupled the area of the central quadrangle and built a superb façade of columns known as the colonnade. He also had the inside decorated, in particular the Apollo gallery.

1793-1814
SUBVERTED
by the Revolution and Napoleon I

After the death of Louis XVI, the Louvre no longer served as a royal palace, and it became a museum instead. The revolutionary government exhibited the royal collections and works of art taken from churches and stately homes. Napoleon I would later extend the museum and give it his name.

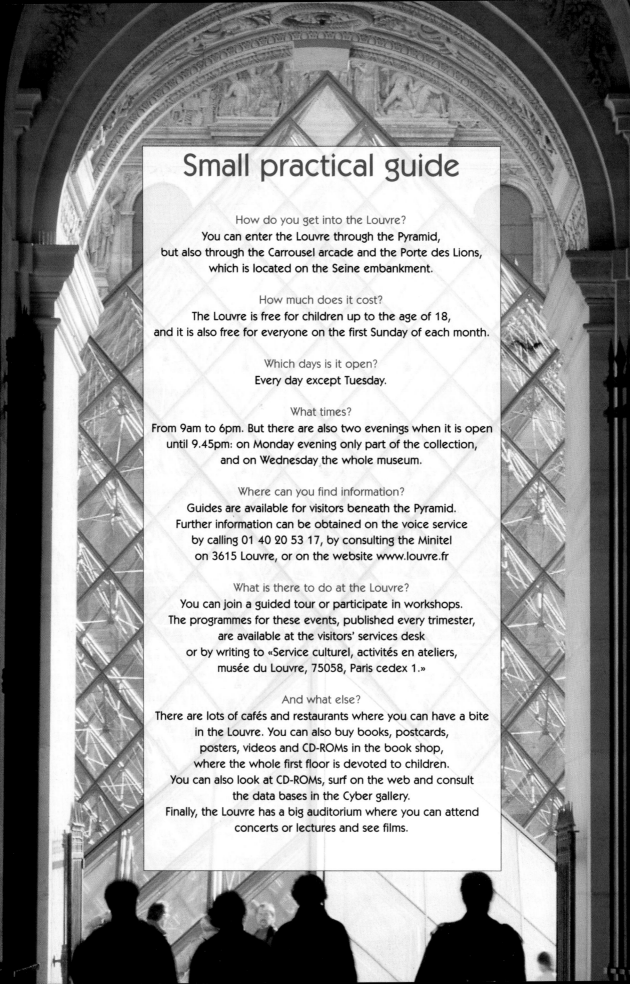

Small practical guide

How do you get into the Louvre?
You can enter the Louvre through the Pyramid,
but also through the Carrousel arcade and the Porte des Lions,
which is located on the Seine embankment.

How much does it cost?
The Louvre is free for children up to the age of 18,
and it is also free for everyone on the first Sunday of each month.

Which days is it open?
Every day except Tuesday.

What times?
From 9am to 6pm. But there are also two evenings when it is open
until 9.45pm: on Monday evening only part of the collection,
and on Wednesday the whole museum.

Where can you find information?
Guides are available for visitors beneath the Pyramid.
Further information can be obtained on the voice service
by calling 01 40 20 53 17, by consulting the Minitel
on 3615 Louvre, or on the website www.louvre.fr

What is there to do at the Louvre?
You can join a guided tour or participate in workshops.
The programmes for these events, published every trimester,
are available at the visitors' services desk
or by writing to «Service culturel, activités en ateliers,
musée du Louvre, 75058, Paris cedex 1.»

And what else?
There are lots of cafés and restaurants where you can have a bite
in the Louvre. You can also buy books, postcards,
posters, videos and CD-ROMs in the book shop,
where the whole first floor is devoted to children.
You can also look at CD-ROMs, surf on the web and consult
the data bases in the Cyber gallery.
Finally, the Louvre has a big auditorium where you can attend
concerts or lectures and see films.